Heaven Cent
Prayers

Anna,
In God We
Trust !
♡ nancy Robert

Heaven Cent Prayers

Nancy Roberts

Pleasant Word
A Division of WinePress Group

Pleasant Word (a division of WinePress Publishing, PO Box 428, Enumclaw, WA 98022) functions only as book publisher. As such, the ultimate design, content, editorial accuracy, and views expressed or implied in this work are those of the author.

All Scripture quotations unless otherwise indicated are taken from the *Good News Translation*—Second Edition. 1992 by American Bible Society. Used by permission.

Scripture quotations marked KJV are taken from the *Holy Bible: King James Version*.

Scripture quotations marked NIV are taken from the *Holy Bible: New International Version*®. NIV®. Copyright © 1973, 1978, 1984 by International Bible Society. Used by permission of Zondervan. All rights reserved.

Scripture quotations marked NLT are taken from the *Holy Bible, New Living Translation,* copyright © 1996. Used by permission of Tyndale House Publishers, Inc., Wheaton, IL 60189 USA. All rights reserved.

Scripture quotations marked NRSV are taken from the *New Revised Standard Version Bible,* copyright 1989, Division of Christian Education of the National Council of the Churches of Christ in the United States of America. Used by permission. All rights reserved.

Scripture quotations marked NKJV are taken from the *New King James Version.* Copyright © 1982 by Thomas Nelson, Inc. Used by permission. All rights reserved.

ISBN 13: 978-1-4141-1200-8
ISBN 10: 1-4141-1200-9
Library of Congress Catalog Card Number: 2009921370

Contents

Introduction

I cannot believe it has been six years since I found that innocent little cent, or maybe it found me. I'd like to thank the person who dropped that penny. How it got under that bench in that particular shopping center at that time, on that day, I will never know, 'cuz it's a God thing. Holding very little monetary value, the lesson the penny taught me holds more value than millions of dollars.

As my husband and I sat together on that bench, we found ourselves waiting . . . waiting for *my* doctor's appointment. You see, ten weeks before, I had been diagnosed with multiple sclerosis, which primarily affected my vision. I had needed to take a leave of absence from my job as a registered nurse in the operating room, and I was hoping for medical clearance to return to my job. As we sat together holding hands on the bench, the thoughts that were running through my mind, and my husband's, were: *What is going to happen to our finances if I can't work? What if I can't drive? What if MS keeps getting worse and worse and I end up in a wheelchair? What if my vision continues to darken?* My list grew longer with each passing moment.

While all these questions swirled around in my head, I looked down at the floor, my eyes brimming with tears, and I spotted the innocent, little penny. It was "heads up," and as I picked it up, I noticed that Abe Lincoln's head had spots on it, probably from all the fingers that had touched it before. I smiled as I thought, *Hey, Abe's got MS too!* (MS causes "spots" in your brain that show up on MRI scans.) But it was the words engraved above Abe's head that jumped out at me. "In God We Trust"—*yes, that's it! We need to trust!* And trust I did—I was able to return to work, and frankly, I'm a better nurse and a more understanding person because I have this health issue. What I've learned through this experience is invaluable.

I started writing six years ago and have not stopped. I thank only the Lord for this. He alone is to be praised for my situation. My goal in writing *Heaven Cent Prayers* is not to put *my* life into the prayers, but for you, my friend, to put your unique life situations into the Lord's hands; He is your friend who can be trusted in every situation. I want to tell you who the Lord is and tell you that He loves to hear from His children. Prayer is our connection to the Lord, and it's how we get to know each other. Watching Him take the situations in our lives, work in them, and finally make "cents" of them is so amazing.

You have in your hands one dollar and one penny's worth of prayers; spend your time wisely, getting to know the Lord and watching Him make changes. I wish you all blessings from the Lord, because "In God We Trust."

—**Nancy Roberts**

CHAPTER 1

Calm

And he arose, rebuked the wind, and said unto the sea, Peace
be still. And the wind ceased, and there was a great calm.
—Mark 4:30

Jesus,

You have power over the wind and waves that stir up
trouble in my life. Today, right now, in this minute, let the
waves of peace wash over my situation, my outlook, and my
attitude. Help me to remember that you steer the ship of my
life. You are the captain. I trust in your control. Nothing fazes
you. Nothing distracts you. May your peace, which transcends
all human understanding, keep me afloat in troubled seas. I rest
in the knowledge that you lead me beside still, quiet waters in
which I find total restoration to calm my soul.

In God we trust,
Amen

CHAPTER 2

Wrath

Fathers, provoke not your children to wrath; but bring them up in the nurture and admonition of the Lord.

—Ephesians 6:4 KJV

Heavenly Father,

You have a son named Jesus. He was perfect in every way. How can you possibly understand what I'm going through? This child is a gift, created from a miracle. Help me not to forget that. I'm trying to raise this child, knowing that you are *our* heavenly Father, who will nurture us both in faith and through all the roadblocks life puts in our way. Parents and children feel "road wrath" as they grow. Help us all, as parents and children, to learn from each other and to have patience prevail in our family. The enemy loves it when we fight; this only breeds anger, sadness, and resentment. The roots of these emotions grow deep into our souls. Heavenly Father, pull them out, and in their place plant tolerance and love. Teach me to nurture my child in your peace.

In God we trust,
Amen

CHAPTER 3

Accomplish

As the rain and snow come down from heaven and do not return to it without watering the earth and making it bud and flourish, so that it yields seeds for the sower and bread for the eater, so is my word that goes out from my mouth: It will not return to me empty, but will accomplish what I desire and achieve the purpose for which I sent it.

—Isaiah 55:10–11 NIV

Creator,

Life is one huge cycle . . . one step after another, designed by an awesome God. Sunrise, sunset, stars, moon, rain—it's all part of your almighty plan. Lord, you set this plan into motion, and you won't just leave us to spin off into space on a decaying planet. You love us and have a purpose for each of us. You fill us every day with blessings from this amazing creation. No person, when he or she feels the wind, touches the dirt, or hears a bird, can deny your existence if he or she has you, Father, safely planted in his or her heart.

Today, as the sun rises and sets, may I accomplish what you have planned for me: not my will, but yours alone be achieved.

In God we trust,
Amen

Hope

And not only that, but we also glory in tribulations, knowing that tribulations produce perseverance; and perseverance, character; and character hope.

—Romans 5:3–4 KJV

Father,

Sometimes I look to the future and I just don't have that hope in my heart. I see the troubles of life: they seem to encompass me, overwhelm me, and distract me. Help me to focus on you and your plan. You alone, Father, are in my future. You know the ending to the story. The ending is definitely a happy one, because I'm placing these troubles and distractions in your hands. I can handle them no longer; yet, I continue to run the race of life, feeling lighter and uplifted. When I cross the finish line of life, I look forward to falling freely into your arms. And I hope, no, I know I will hear the words of approval from my heavenly Father, "Well done, the race is finished, enter eternity my child."

In God I trust,
Amen

CHAPTER 5

Know

Be still, and know that I am God.

—Psalm 46:10 KJV

Lord God,

What do I know? Not much it seems. I try and try to do what I think is right, and no! That door is shut, slammed shut right in my face, right in front of me. I can feel the rush of air as the door flies shut and the crash of the wood as it hits the frame. You know, Lord, with the door shut, it's quiet in here . . . I can think. Maybe that was your goal all along. I'm in a spiritual "time out" right now. Yes, I had a temper tantrum. I'm angry that your answer to this situation is "no," but I do know that I'm not alone in this room. As I turn my face from the corner and face you, I see an open window. There is a better answer to this situation. It is in your will that I need to trust, not in my willful nature that's driving me to be in a sulky anger. I'm disappointed, yet you have provided me with a way to deal with this situation. I don't directly see the answer yet, but the light of your love shines through the window in my pouting soul. Father, Abba, I'm sorry . . . can you forgive your willful child? I know in my heart I'm forgiven.

In God I trust,
Amen

CHAPTER 6

Cold

He gives a command to the earth, and what he says is quickly
done. He spreads snow like a blanket and scatters frost like
dust. He sends hail like gravel; no one can endure the cold
He sends! Then He gives a command, and the ice melts; He
sends the wind and the water flows.

—Psalm 147:15–18

Lord,

As I pray today, it is fifteen degrees below zero. The sky is
crystal blue, with the sun piercing through the cold air. The sun
is powerless today to melt the snow, but it's shining through
my window, and its rays provide warmth in my home. Today,
Jesus, I lift a thank you heavenward for my earthly home. Many
throughout the earth have no home. Jesus, as you walked on
this earth, you didn't have a home either. You relied on the
open doors and hearts of people. Jesus, while I appreciate the
earthly home you have blessed my family with, help me to also
share my blessings with others. As your love warms my heart,
help me to warm the lives of others with generosity. Help me,
Jesus, not to be cold-hearted; let your love warm my actions
into loving deeds. Show me where I can be of service.

> In God we trust to warm us,
> Amen

CHAPTER 7

Confidence

Cast not away therefore your confidence, which hath great recompense of reward. For ye have need of patience, that, after ye have done the will of God, ye might receive the promise.

—Hebrews 10:35–36 KJV

Lord,

Some days I feel like I'm on the right course. Other times I feel blown about by the wind—by the opinions of others that they so lovingly feel they need to voice. I know you talk through others, but, Lord, which voice is yours? I do know this: if I *first* step out in faith, I will hear your voice, and I will know in my heart that I have done the right thing. If it is wrong, well, you will be there for me then too. The key is *faith*. When I think about it, the words "faith" and "confidence" are just about the same. Faith is taking a step forward; confidence knows there is a floor underneath you to put your foot on. Confidence knows there's a floor, but faith is taking a step forward. It works either way. Father, as I take a step forward, I feel you grasp my hand. I am confident that even if I fall, as long as I keep holding your hand, I'm okay. I trust completely in you.

In God I trust,
Amen

CHAPTER 8

Safe

The Lord is my protector; He is my strong fortress. My God is my Protection, and with Him I am safe. He protects me like a shield; he defends me and keeps me safe.

—Psalm 18:2

Lord,

On earth I feel so vulnerable . . .
Are the kids safe when they go to school?
Is my family safe in my home?
Are the roads safe to drive on?
Is the Internet a safe place to find information,
    or will somebody find me first?
Are the foods we consume safe?
Are my investments safe?
Is it safe to breathe the air?
Is it safe to be in the sunshine?
Is my job safe?
Lord, I have so many questions . . . I know I can always go to you in prayer for the answers. I do not need a road, an Internet connection, electricity, or fuel to connect with you. All I do is quiet my spinning thoughts, find peace in your promises, and rest in the safety that only you provide. Keep me grounded in you.

In God alone I put my trust,
Amen

CHAPTER 9

Value

Fear not therefore, ye are of more value than many sparrows.

—Matthew 10:31 KJV

Father God,

In today's world, value is all relative. It all depends on what you hold dear. One person might look at a garage sale and say, "junk"; another might find a hidden treasure there. Value is in the eyes of the beholder. Today I saw a flock of sparrows hiding in a small clump of bushes as I left the store. They caught my eye, and I remember smiling. I thought to myself, *How dirty they look*. It's winter here, and everything looks dingy, including these hardy birds, who can actually survive these temperatures. I went back, Father, and read more of Matthew 10. In the Good News Version it says in verses 29–30, "For only a penny you can buy two sparrows, yet not one sparrow falls to the ground without your Father's consent. As for you, even the hairs of your head have all been counted." Father, I think this is the only place a penny is mentioned in the Bible. A penny isn't very valuable, neither is a sparrow, but you say in your Word that I'm more valuable. You even know me personally, so even my hairs each have a number. Father, as I look at a penny, I understand value. I'm valuable to you. I needed to know that. You are valuable, no *vital*, to my existence too. Thank you for reminding me of this.

In God we trust,
Amen

CHAPTER 10

Mind

Do not conform yourselves to the standards of this world, but let God transform you inwardly by a complete change of your mind. Then you will be able to know the will of God—what is pleasing to him and is perfect.

—Romans 12:2

Holy Spirit,

Today I give my mind/thoughts/desires completely to you. I let go of the world's way and surrender totally to your will. I want to know what pleases you, because your will is perfect. Holy One, I wrestle with this. I hold on to the world's unimportant standards. Your will, timing, and ways are perfect. I ask you humbly, Holy Spirit, to light a fire in my will so that it burns in sync with you. May this fire light my path for the future. Even though this may not be the popular way to go, I don't mind. Change me completely, totally, and without reservation.

In the Holy Spirit I trust,
Amen

CHAPTER 11

Requires

No, the Lord has told us what is good. What he requires of us is this: To do what is just, to show constant love, and to live in humble fellowship with God.

—Micah 6:8

Dearest God,

What you require seems simple on paper, but it is very difficult to put in practice in my daily life.

1. Be fair.
2. Love always.
3. Live humbly.

Micah wrote these words in the Old Testament, but they were made alive by Jesus and the life he lived here on earth. My humble attempt at putting these three goals into practice seems *futile*; yet, through faith in you, I can move mountains. What you require is my love. God, I have accepted you totally in my heart. Transform me into a "doer" of your Word and not a person who sits on the sidelines. God, put me in the game. I'll play hard, and I'll do my absolute best. God, what will you require of me today?

In God we trust,
Amen

CHAPTER 12

Appreciation

Listen to your father, without him you would not exist.
When your mother's old, show her your appreciation.

—Proverbs 23:22

Father,

As parents age, it's hard to appreciate them. I ask for help in this matter. We are *all* your children. Help me to see my parents through your eyes—see them as having weathered parenting themselves. Father, help me to appreciate where they've been, where they are now, and where they are going. Their journey has been a long one, and for this I thank you. I thank you also for the fact that they raised me to know you. They raised me the best they could, not perfect—that's impossible, nobody's perfect. May all their shortcomings and frailties be cloaked with the goodness and memories they provided. People change, times change, life changes, but you, heavenly Father, *never* change. Lord, you love all your children with a timeless quality that I thank you for. I appreciate you in the lives of my parents and your presence in my own life as well. Help me never to forget where I came from—parents who helped me love you.

In God I trust,
Amen

Grace

Let us come boldly unto the throne of grace that we may
obtain mercy, and find grace to help in time of need.

—Hebrews 4:16 KJV

Sweet Jesus,

I approach your throne, totally undeserving, yet boldly
seeking grace. Am I in need? Yes, Jesus, 24/7, I'm in need of
you. I can't and won't go at this undertaking alone. You walk
with me. You show me the way. Jesus, I want and have to share
your grace with others in my life. Be my hands, feet, voice,
eyes, and ears. Soak through my will. Give me grace to see
others in need, hear their cries for help, wipe away any tears,
and offer my hands and feet to do what is required. Amazing
grace . . . amazing grace . . . how sweet the sound . . . .

In God I trust,
Amen

CHAPTER 14

Wait

Wait for the Lord; be strong and take heart and wait for the Lord.

—Psalm 27:14 NIV

Father,

I'm not good at this waiting stuff. Patience is not one of my strong points. I like to move and get 'er done! You tell me to be strong and take heart. My heart is strong—I work out, I eat right . . . but that's not what you mean. Father, my heart is very heavy. I'm tired of carrying this weight of worry. Wait . . . weight . . . wait. Father, on this earth I'm in heaven's waiting room—I'm waiting to see you, and I will someday, but you have a plan for me and my family. So as I wait, I turn and look—hey, there's a book on the coffee table. I reach for it, hold it, look at it, open it. Hey, Father, it's the Bible; the answer was here all along. Psalm 31:24 says, "Be strong and take heart, all you who hope in the Lord." You are repeating yourself, and the word that *jumps* out at my eyes is "hope." Yes, Lord, you have given me hope! I will wait with hope in my heart. You are an awesome God! Thank you!

In God I trust with hope,
Amen

CHAPTER 15

Tears

I have heard thy prayer, I have seen thy tears, behold I will
heal thee.

—2 Kings 20:5 KJV

Lord,

They say your eyes are the windows to your soul.
Seems my body is closing the drapes.
Without my vision, I'm not quite whole.
From this plight I need an escape.
With my mind I still think, with my hand I still write.
My thoughts and words like a bird take flight.
On a wing and a prayer my words are still scratched out.
My writing is sloppy, but there is no doubt
That God is still there, though my eyes cannot see.
My heart is set on His will for me.
So this is happening, I do not ask why.
My vision is failing, but my eyes can still cry.
Seeing through the tears is my mission and goal.
I feel this fully with my heart and soul.
No one knows the future, but it only looks dim,
If we take our eyes and stop looking at Him.

In God we trust,
Amen

CHAPTER 16

Abandon

"Eloi, Eloi, lama sabachthani?"—which means, "My God, my God, why have you forsaken me?"

—Matthew 27:46 NIV

Jesus,

> You felt abandoned by your Father . . .
> His heart must have been broken . . .
> Your body was broken . . .
> People have broken your heart by the hardness of their own hearts.
> Jesus, please don't abandon me.
> My heart is broken too.
> I need you to restore my heart.
> You promise to be with me until time as we know it ends.
> This brings an end to my loneliness.
> In the end you alone mend the heart of your friend.

In Jesus I, _____, trust,

(please sign your name)

Amen

CHAPTER 17

Plans

I alone know the plans I have for you, plans to bring you prosperity and not disaster, plans to bring about the future you hope for.

—Jeremiah 29:11

Savior,

I plan my day. I plan my grocery list. I plan my retirement. I plan what to wear. Somehow this all seems trivial because you alone know the plan, the master plan for my salvation. As far as the future is concerned, only you know what is out there. My human brain can't take it all in sometimes. When you told Jeremiah you were bringing him prosperity, I don't think you meant wealth in the earthly terms. Your plan is more thorough. You are a multipurpose God. You can accomplish many things with just one situation. Save me from thinking your plans involve me alone. Your plans involve all who believe in you. Our hope lies in you. You, Savior, are what we hope for.

You may make plans, but God directs your actions.

—Proverbs 16:9

In our Savior we trust,
Amen

CHAPTER 18

Smiling

Smiling faces make you happy, and good news makes you feel better.

—Proverbs 15:30

Lord,

Sometimes I wonder if, when you look at us from heaven, you are happy or sad. While there are a lot of bad things going on today, Lord, it's my goal to make you smile. Now, I know we were created in your image, so I bet we as humans can make you laugh too. Today, through my actions, I pray I will make you smile, Lord. Smiling is contagious. Today I will spread cheer.

In God I trust to make this so,
Amen

CHAPTER 19

Nothing

I am the vine, you are the branches. Whoever remains in me
and I in him, will bear much fruit; for you can do nothing
without me.

—John 15:5

Lord God,

Sometimes I feel like nothing is happening in my life and
your plan for it. I feel stale, useless, and stagnant. I'm a seed
underground during the winter, waiting to sprout; yet I don't
feel that spring warmth pushing me into action and growth. I
feel nothing, Lord. I can be patient and wait for the warmth of
your love to add life to the soil of my situation. I want to see
and feel movement, change, and light. I remain in nothingness.
You are here though, aren't you, Lord? Can we just be together
right here, right now? Lord, I reach out . . . take my hand. Can
we just sit here in your peace? It's so quiet. I see nothing, feel
nothing, hear . . . wait . . . I can hear my heart. It's a miracle
that it beats every minute of every day. You put my heart into
motion, Lord. You've put my life in motion. God, you make
miracles happen with every beat of my heart. My heart beats
on, and so does life. My heart is connected to miles of vessels
that carry blood to every part of me. They branch out, and so
will I, Lord, when you say the time is right. I can do nothing
without you, Lord. Help me to remain patient.

> In God I trust that spring
> will arrive,
> Amen

CHAPTER 20

Fear

Where God's love is, there is no fear. God's perfect love takes away fear. It is punishment that makes a person fear. Anyone who has fear does not have perfect love.

—1 John 4:18–19

Lord,

Fear of the future and of what lies ahead,
I don't know about tomorrow,
    is there something to dread?
I sometimes lose sleep, and my hair's turning gray.
There are kids to raise and bills to pay.
I punish myself by thinking this way,
When the answer is this,
Pray, pray, pray, pray!
I take all my worries, Lord. I pray them to you.
You know my heart, Lord, and you'll help me through.
I lay my worries all at your throne.
In my faith walk, you won't leave me out on my own.
Replace all those fears in the deepest parts of my soul.
With your love so perfect, Lord God,
    please make me whole.
Work out situations and do what you must.

I love you completely, and
in God I trust,
Amen

CHAPTER 21

Boast

The Lord says, "Wise men should not boast of their wisdom, or strong men of their strength, or rich men of their wealth. If anyone wants to boast, he should boast that he knows and understands me, because my love is constant, and I do what is just and right. These are the things that please me. I the Lord have spoken."

—Jeremiah 9:23–24

Mighty God,

Jeremiah really hit the nail right on the head when he wrote this. This passage is fitting to read before going to a party or a gathering of people. We have the human need to be noticed. We get all dressed up; we talk of our jobs and families. We are proud—God, help me to be proud of you. You made me who I am. You blessed me. Your love is constant, not like earthly "stuff" that can go away overnight. In situations where I meet new people, God, place me in conversations that please you. In fact, be the gatekeeper of my mouth, so I say and do what pleases you. Turn my boasting into confidence and bragging into listening.

In Almighty, all-knowing,
all-powerful God
I put my trust,
Amen

CHAPTER 22

Possible

With men this is impossible, but with God all things are possible.

—Matthew 19:26 NIV

Lord God,

What is possible today? All things! Lord, this world is full of the superficial and artificial, making anything seem possible. But that's just it—things only *seem* possible. They aren't real if we rely on what the world tells us. Lord, you are full of possibilities, and they are endless because you are almighty and all powerful. You think of things that we can't possibly imagine in our little brains. Help me today, Lord, to turn the seemingly impossible into I'm possible. I am possible.

You are the "I AM." Help me to realize the possibilities you place before me each and every day.

In God, who makes all things
possible, I trust,
Amen

Do

Whatever you do, do well.

—Ecclesiastes 9:10 NIV

God,

Have you ever tried to do something and you think you've done well, only to find out it was not right in someone else's opinion and there wasn't one right way to begin with and everybody's telling you what they think you should do and—wait a minute, you're God! Your way is always done well, perfectly, in fact. God, I don't see the big picture right now. I know I don't have to. But what if my best isn't good enough? Father, I'm such a perfectionist. What I think I need is a thicker skin. I'll develop that only through the onslaught of criticism. God, I will do my best and let you handle the rest.

In God I do trust,
Amen

CHAPTER 24

Heal

I have heard thy prayer. I have seen thy tears; behold. I will heal thee.

—2 Kings 20:5

Jesus,

You, in your walk on this earth, healed so many. Lord, I'm feeling so bad. I pray for your healing. Our bodies are miracles, the way you created them. They are able to fight off disease: My body is fighting with all it's got to battle the germs we can't even see. These invaders will be overcome; it will just take time. I'm using this time to pray. I'm here alone because I don't want to give these germs to others. Jesus, I rest in you—rest is what my body needs, and my soul as well. I rest in your healing embrace.

In Jesus, the healer, I trust,
Amen

CHAPTER 25

Faith

To have faith is to be sure of the things we hope for, to be certain of the things we cannot see.

—Hebrews 11:1

Holy One,

There have been situations in my life that have definitely shaken my faith. All these situations have, in the end, made me a stronger person. When I'm going through tough times and I cannot see the light at the end of the tunnel, help me to know it's there. Hope keeps me going and faith makes me take the steps. I reach out for you in utter darkness sometimes; I am sure of your presence. I feel your love in my heart. My heart is beating, Lord, I will get through. Show me the way, even when it's too dark to see. Faith in you, Holy One, is the hope in my steps.

In the Holy One I trust,
Amen

CHAPTER 26

Persistent

Be persistent in prayer, and keep alert as you pray, giving thanks to God.

—Colossians 4:2

Everlasting God,

Sometimes when I pray, I wonder how many people are praying at the same time—probably millions. How do you keep it all straight? I guess I'll ask you that question when I get to heaven. Lord, sometimes I feel like I'm asking for the same things over and over. I'm persistent all right, but what about being alert? I'm afraid I fall asleep sometimes, like the disciples did in the garden of Gethsemane. Lord, I thank you for not keeping track of this. I want to lift up a thank you for being there in the past, walking with me now, and leading me to a future, our future, where you are with me. I ask only for your hand, Holy One, to lead me (but I will keep praying every day and probably ask you for the same things anyway).

In my everlasting God
I put my trust,
Amen

CHAPTER 27

Number

Teach us to number our days, that we may apply our hearts unto wisdom.

—Psalm 90:12 KJV

Father, how many days do I have on this earth? No one knows but you, my friend. Help me to make each day count. Every day, teach me something new. Help me to have an open mind to learn more and more. Father, help me to apply what I've been taught, especially from loved ones who have gone before me. I know how much my heart is saddened when loved ones die, but help me to focus on the days they had and how we learned from their lives. Father, it could be hours, days, or years before I die, but I rest in your promise of heaven. I look forward to being with all the saints who have gone before me. I will take a moment to number those I love who are already with you right now.

Father, there are some amazing saints in heaven with you! I'll get there someday too . . . .

In God we trust,
Amen

CHAPTER 28

Rock

So then, anyone who hears these words of mine and obeys them is like a wise man who built his house on a rock. The rain poured down, the rivers flooded over, and the wind blew hard against that house. But it did not fall, it was built on rock. But anyone who hears these words of mine and does not obey them is like a foolish man who built his house on sand. The rain poured down, the rivers flooded over, the wind blew hard against that house and it fell. And what a terrible fall it was!

—Matthew 7:24–27

Jesus,

You are the rock I want to build the foundation of my faith on. I feel pummeled often by the storms of this world, by the flood of trends, by the waves of panic, by the thunder of lies from the enemy. I cling tightly to you, listening to and reading your words. Thank you for telling parables to me, Jesus. I know your words were spoken long ago, but they are as true and valuable today as the day you spoke them. Jesus, help me to keep my house in order, founded on your love, weathered from storms, but standing firm in a faith that is rock solid.

> In Jesus, the Rock, I put my
> trust,
> Amen

CHAPTER 29

Precious

> I will give up whole nations to save your life, because you are precious to me and because I love you and give you honor. Do not be afraid—I am with you.
>
> —Isaiah 43:4–5

God,

You tell me I am precious, and to me that means so much. I don't feel of value many days—but that's by earthly standards. You say you love me too. I desperately needed to hear that as well. You are always with me; I will try not to be afraid. There are three promises in this passage from Isaiah that I see, and they reveal to me who you are.

1. I give.
2. I love.
3. I Am.

If the "I Am," the God of the universe, loves me and gives me honor because I am precious to him, then my life is worth a great deal—more than I can ever imagine. Abba, you are precious to me too.

In the "I Am" we trust,
Amen

CHAPTER 30

Armor

Finally, build up your strength in union with the Lord and by means of his mighty power. Put on all the armor that God gives you, so that you will be able to stand up against the devil's evil tricks. For we are not fighting against human beings but against the wicked spiritual forces in the heavenly world, the rulers, authorities, and cosmic powers of this Dark Age. So put on God's armor now! Then when the evil day comes, you will be able to resist the enemy's attacks, and after fighting to the end, you will still hold your ground. So stand ready with truth as a belt tight around your waist, with righteousness as your breastplate, and as your shoes the readiness to announce the good news of peace. And at all times carry faith as a shield; for it will be able to put out all the burning arrows shot by the evil one. And accept salvation as a helmet, and the Word of God as a sword which the spirit gives you. Do all this in prayer, asking for God's help. Pray on every occasion as the Spirit leads, for this reason keep alert and never give up, pray always for God's people.

—Ephesians 6:10–18

Today, Father, as I get dressed I say a prayer,
For Father, your outfit is exactly what I should wear.
I put on my shirt as a good place to start,
Remembering that righteousness covers my heart.
I put on a belt, with truth at my waist.
This keeps me honest and holds everything in place.
I don a hat on this head with my logic.
Protect my thoughts, may they follow your projects.

For my feet I put on shoes that are ready to do,
And in my hand a shield of faith that reflects the whole
 day through.
And in my other, still empty hand
I'll carry your Word, and with it I'll stand
Firm in whatever comes my way,
For I have all the armor I need for today.

> In God we trust,
> Amen.

CHAPTER 31

Protect

I look to the mountains; where will my help come from? My help will come from the Lord, who made heaven and earth. He will not let you fall; your protector is always awake. The protector of Israel never dozes or sleeps. The Lord will guard you; he is by your side to protect you. The sun will not hurt you during the day, nor the moon during the night. The Lord will protect you from all danger; he will protect you as you come and go now and forever.

—Psalm 121:1–8

Father God, you never sleep.
You watch over me and safely keep
Me from dangers,
Both obvious and unseen.
You're my guide and crutch; on you I lean.
Fill me with courage and confidence today.
Protect me from dangers,
And show me the way.

In God alone I trust,
Amen

CHAPTER 32

Praise

I will praise you, Lord, with all my heart; I will tell of all the
wonderful things you have done.

—Psalm 9:1

Lord,

As the sun comes up on a new day and sheds light, ending
the night time, so may it be with my perspective today. Shine
a ray of light into my heart. Lord, I raise this prayer of praise
to you. I will ponder all the amazing things that have been ac-
complished through you. I will take this moment to remember
them now . . . . All these memories, I take with me to help me
never to forget these wonderful things. I'll move forward and
start today feeling renewed.

In God I trust and praise,
Amen

CHAPTER 33

Transform

Do not conform yourselves to the standards of the world, but let God transform you inwardly by a complete change of your mind, then you will be able to know the will of God—what is good and is pleasing to him and is perfect.

—Romans 12:2

God,

You gave me this brain.
You gave me this mind.
You made me think.

Transform what is in my mind to what is pleasing to you. Take my thoughts, God. May they focus on the good in this world. You created us in your image—open my mind so that I see your image in others. God, where can I help my fellow humans on this earth? Show me where I can serve others, and in so doing, may I serve you as well. Transform me from a hinderer to a helper. Transform me from an observer to a participant. Transform me from passive to active. Take my will and make it yours.

In God I trust,
Amen

CHAPTER 34

Leap

Give strength to hands that are tired, and to knees that
tremble with weakness. Tell everyone who is discouraged,
"Be strong and don't be afraid! God is coming to your res-
cue, coming to punish your enemies." The blind will be able
to see, and the deaf will hear. The lame will leap and dance
and those who cannot speak will shout for joy.

—Isaiah 35:3–6

God,

Everyone who's ever felt tired, exhausted, used up, or
weak, or has battled a disability or sickness, had nothing left,
or couldn't take another step, Isaiah mentions in this passage.
That's everybody! We all need to take a leap of faith here, don't
we, Father? Today is leap day, February 29, 2008. I feel encour-
aged as I read this passage, especially today! You cheer me on,
Lord, and I in turn, will encourage others to take a leap of faith
as well. We all need to be cheerleaders for each other. Good
attitudes are contagious!

> In God we trust in a leap
> of faith,
> Amen

CHAPTER 35

Endurance

My brothers and sisters, whenever you face trials of any kind, consider it nothing but joy, because you know that the testing of your faith produces endurance; and let endurance have its full effect, so that you may be mature and complete, lacking nothing.

—James 1:2–4 NRSV

Eternal God,

I'm in this for the long haul . . . . The testing of life's circumstances is not over in the blink of an eye. This is a lifelong process. I'm supposed to look at this testing with joy; that's really hard to do, Lord. Help me to have a fresh perspective on this race of life. Not only are you waiting at the finish line, but also you, God, keep me going in this marathon. There will be uphill battles, but they only help me appreciate the downhill rides. Life will throw us curves, but I'm energized to see what's around the bend. Faith in you produces the endurance I need to complete this race.

In God I trust to keep me going,
Amen

Goal

So we make it our goal to please Him.

—2 Corinthians 5:9

Lord,

What is my goal? Just by writing down these prayers, I'm working toward what is my personal hope and goal: to publish *Making Sense? Heaven Cent Prayers? Pennies from Heaven?* (I don't even know if that is the title I'm going to use.) This is only #36; I have 64 prayers left to write! You and I can do this, Lord! I just need to keep at it. (And to whoever's eyes focus on these words right now—you can do it too! What are *your* goals? Long term, I mean—by what do you want to be remembered? By talking with the Lord, that's how I am accomplishing my goal. I'm a communicator of sorts—give me a pen, and away I go.) This prayer is for anyone who reads this. Set the bar high—in the heavens perhaps. You and God can accomplish great things, if only you both set the goals together.

In God we trust,
Amen

CHAPTER 37

Pray

But when you pray, do not be like the hypocrites! They love to stand up and pray in the houses of worship and on street corners, so that everyone can see them. I assure you they have already been paid in full. But when you pray, go to your room, close the door, and pray to your Father, who is unseen. And your Father, who sees what you do in private will reward you.

—Matthew 6:6

Jesus,

There's a feeling of togetherness when I pray with fellow members of the body of Christ at our church. Do you hear those prayers more than when I'm praying all by myself in the car on my morning commute to work or when I'm at home in the evening while sitting in the quiet? You hear all prayers, Lord. I enjoy my prayer time so much. It's just the two of us sitting here, having a conversation. That's the way prayer is: a two-way conversation. At times I feel I'm talking, asking, talking, demanding, talking.

> I'm not listening. That is why we need this quiet place to talk.
> I need to hear you, Jesus.
> The noise of life in this world is so loud sometimes.
> I need to hear you, Jesus.
> Life is so busy; I forget to ask you to be a part of my day.
> I need to hear you, Jesus.

Chaos is everywhere; the energy from this
creates more confusion.
    I need to hear you, Jesus.
My to-do list is long, and my time is short.
    I need to hear you, Jesus.
When my heart is heavy with burdens galore,
    I need to hear you, Jesus.
When my heart is light with praise for you,
    I need to hear you, Jesus.
I am here in your presence…listening…quiet…peaceful…
    I need to hear you, Jesus.

                In Jesus I trust,
                Amen

CHAPTER 38

Cross

If any of you wants to be my follower, you must put aside selfish ambitions, shoulder your cross and follow me. If you try to keep your life for yourself, you will lose it. But if you give up your life for me, you will find true life.

—Matthew 16:24–25 NLT

Jesus,

You shouldered that heavy cross up Calvary's hill.
You were obedient completely to your Father's will.
Friends mocked you and laughed, soldiers drew
    lots for your clothes.
The pain in your hands and feet,
No human knows.
Unimaginable cross, made from a tree,
Holding my Savior for all to see.
You conquered evil and banished the foe.
You did this for all,
And you want us to know
That the cross is a symbol of sacrifice and love.
My Jesus reigns victorious in heaven above.

In Jesus we trust,
Amen

CHAPTER 39

Overcame

He who overcomes I will grant to him to sit down with me on my throne, as I also overcame and sat down with my father on his throne.

—Revelation 3:24 KJV

Jesus,

To sit down and talk with you in heaven is my goal. I have so many questions for you. Jesus, you overcame sin by dying on the cross and rising from the dead. What an honor it will be to actually sit down and discuss everything in this way. You help me overcome my obstacles here on earth; I can only do this with you at my side and in my heart. I believe that while you were here on earth, you were tested and tempted in every way as I am now in my life. You won the victory! We are a winning team! Jesus, help me be victorious too, so we'll do the victory dance in heaven together!

In Jesus we trust,
Amen

CHAPTER 40

Fix

Fix your thoughts on what is true and honorable and right.
—Philippians 4:8 NLT

Jesus,

Joseph, your earthly father, was a carpenter. I bet he taught you about hammers, nails, and how to fix things. Jesus, today I ask you to fix my thoughts on you alone! You are the way, the truth, and the life (John 14:6). The enemy comes in and tries to scramble my thoughts, so I'm focused on the wrong things or on trivial things or on lies that he whispers in my ear. Jesus, the devil came and tested you in these ways too. Cover my thoughts in the blanket of truth. Fix it so that the enemy has no way into my thoughts; his misguided logic has no home in my head. I cannot do this on my own. But more importantly, I have faith in you, Jesus, to fix this.

In Jesus, my Handyman,
I trust,
Amen

CHAPTER 41

Crooked

Consider what God has done: who can straighten what he has made crooked? When times are good be happy but when times are bad consider: God has made the one as well as the other. Therefore, a man cannot discover anything about his future.

—Ecclesiastes 7:13–14 NIV

Lord,

Life isn't fashioned to be a straight shot to the top—is it, Lord? No, life is sometimes a crooked mess that no one seems to be able to figure out; but that's just it . . . we need you. Lord, I need you. I give you my maze of thoughts, nest of troubles, and tangle of worries. Take the crooked knot and untangle the web, Lord. I'll keep hanging on to your hand for guidance. I won't hang on to the tangled problem, though; that's up to you. Lord, I give you this yarn; help me to make something wonderful with it—something beautiful. Help me to learn from the past knots and mistakes and weave them with time into something I can be truly proud of. I'll show people my life, but more importantly, your handiwork woven in it. Lord, thank you for setting me straight.

In God I trust,
Amen

CHAPTER 42

Shows

My children, our love should not be just words and talk; it must be true love, which shows itself in action.

—1 John 3:18

Holy Father,

I am your child. Help me not just to talk of your greatness, but help me to show others by how I live my life. Father, I have a job to do. You have assigned me to complete it. I am totally available to you and your will. Show me the way, because your timing is perfect. Sometimes you give me a glimpse of what is to be, Father. It's like a package waiting to be unwrapped. I don't mean to be impatient; I'm just ready, willing, and able for action. Father, put me to work.

In my Father I trust,
Amen

CHAPTER 43

Purpose

We know that all things work together for good with those who love him; those whom he has called according to his purpose.

—Romans 8:28

Lord,

Some situations seemingly have no purpose. For example, why do some people die young? I've always wanted to ask you this. A friend of mine died before she even got a chance to go to college to be a teacher. Lord, I remember her death, her funeral. I even dreamt about her at that time. But now, Lord, I don't remember having any dreams about her for a very long time. She never got the chance to get married, have children, graduate from school, buy a house, travel, see the world—all those great things in life. Why, Lord? What's the purpose? Romans 8:28 was read at her funeral. Lord, you called her home. I'm remembering her today. Weave this experience, Father, into the fabric of my life so that I can learn from it—learn how to grieve, share my experience, and help others in the grief process. I know that she's with you and that heaven is real. Lord, this may sound weird, but can you give her a hug from me? Thank you, Father.

In God I trust,
Amen

CHAPTER 44

Friends

I cannot call you servants any longer, because a servant cannot know what his master is doing. Instead I call you friends, because I have told you everything I heard from my father. You did not choose me, I chose you and appointed you to go and bear much fruit, the kind of fruit that endures. And so the Father will give you whatever you ask of him in my name. This, then, is what I command you; Love one another.

—John 15:15–17

Dear Friend Jesus,

It makes my heart so happy to hear you say we are friends. I can tell you everything. I trust you. You have chosen me too, and I am truly honored by this. We respect each other. We talk to each other. We meet together in prayer. You help me, through the Holy Spirit, to know the Father. What a cool relationship! I treasure this. We stick together in the good times and in the bad. Jesus, I also treasure my friends here on earth. Help me to reach out to them as you do with me. As the old hymn says, "What a friend we have in Jesus, all my sins and griefs to bear, what a privilege to carry, everything to God in prayer." Thank you, Friend.

In my Friend I trust,
Amen

CHAPTER 45

Clothe

You are the people of God; he loved you and chose you for his own. So then you must clothe your selves with compassion, kindness, humility, gentleness and patience.
—Colossians 3:12 NKJV

Lord,

I open my closet in the morning to get dressed. Help me to remember to get dressed in the proper attitude, not just in the clothes I wear. As I put my arms through sleeves, help me to have compassion in my heart if a friend needs a hug. As I put on pants, help me to remember that every step should be taken in a gentle manner. May my coat be a cloak of humbleness. As I put each foot in a shoe, may the footprints I leave behind me be gentle and patient today. Lord, I move forward into the day you have planned for me. I am ready to roll up my sleeves and get to work. Help my attitude to reflect these qualities:

- Humility
- Gentleness
- Compassion
- Kindness
- Patience

> And off I go with the Lord
> I trust to make it so,
> Amen

CHAPTER 46

Doubt

But if any of you lacks wisdom he should pray to God who will give it to him; because God gives generously to all. But when you pray you must believe and not doubt at all. Whoever doubts is a wave on the sea that is driven and blown by the wind.

—James 1:5–6

God,

Sometimes I just feel stupid. I doubt my ability. Lord, you tell me here in James that I can simply pray for wisdom and that You are generous and gracious and will answer my plea. One thing I never doubt is you. You are always the solid anchor in a stormy sea. I doubt myself, but never you. God, I'm not asking for higher intelligence or ability—I'm asking for the knowledge that I can believe in, that is steady, unyielding, and steadfast. I'm not asking for IQ; I'm asking for ND—No Doubt. God, help me to be proud of the person you created me to be—and not to doubt your belief in me. God, you sent your only Son to die on the cross to save me. Your plan was and is secure—no doubts.

In God I trust,
Amen

CHAPTER 47

Gift

Every good gift and every perfect present comes from heaven; it comes down from God, the creator of the heavenly lights, who does not change or cause darkness by turning.

—James 1:16

Creator,

Every day is a gift from you. One size fits all—twenty-four hours is all each one of us has. It's how we use that gift that matters. What will I do today? I will spend my gift wisely. You, Creator of the universe who never changes, are giving me this gift free of charge, with no strings attached. Every day, we have twenty-four hours in which to do our best, rest, and be blessed. Creator, enlighten me so that I can spend this new day in the light of your will, in the light of your creation. There are no shadows, nothing to block the light of seemingly a million birthday candles—candles that are burning for millions of people who are living in your creation. This perfect gift comes solely from you. I thank you for another day.

In our Creator, God, we trust,
Amen

CHAPTER 48

Generations

Now that I am old and my hair is turning grey, do not abandon me, O, God! Be with me while I proclaim your power and might to all generations to come.

—Psalm 71:18

Timeless God,

We are the X generation, the Y generation, and the Baby Boomers. We have fought wars, protested wars, and lost loved ones in battles. We are children, parents, moms, dads, and grandparents. We are young, middle-aged, and old. We are all your people, living out our lives in endless stages, all overlapping and intertwining. God, time is really only a measurement we humans put on things—you are unaffected by it. Every generation thinks it is the first, best, and most progressive. In actuality, God, we all need one another to learn from and to teach. Generations of people are recorded in your Word. Generations are living on earth, and generations are with you, God, in heaven. I have many questions to ask you, God, but for now, I'm satisfied to teach my children and future grandchildren of your timeless love, evidenced by the continuation of life itself. Help me and my generation to be good examples for the future generations.

In the timeless God we trust,
Amen

CHAPTER 49

Written

Now there are many other things that Jesus did. If they were all written down one by one I suppose that the whole world could not hold the books that would be written.

—John 21:25

Jesus,

You have left an imprint on my life. Your hand is shaping me today, as I write this prayer. Jesus, my life seems very insignificant and unworthy; yet I do not truly believe that. My pen touches this paper today for the sole purpose of communicating with you. What I feel you are saying in my heart is "Keep writing, keep listening, keep talking." Jesus, I will tell them who you are. Whoever's eyes fall upon this page, I lift up in this humble prayer. We all want to know you better, Jesus. It's not me that I want people to know, it's you, Jesus. You made us who we are. We carry your love in our hearts. It is written there, and no earthly force can erase it. No one can take your holy words, written in the Bible. Jesus, you were and are alive on earth—make the words come alive today; for they are lovingly written on our hearts.

In Jesus we trust,
Amen

CHAPTER 50

Joy

The joy of the Lord is your strength.

—Nehemiah 8:10 KJV

Lord,

The joy of the Lord is my strength.
The joy of the Lord makes me stronger.
I'm stronger because of the joy of the Lord.
I'm strongest because of the joy of the Lord in my heart.
My heart is strongest when the joy of the Lord is in it.
My heart overflows with the joy of the Lord.
May the joy of the Lord flow from my heart,
   to my hands to share with others,
So the joy of the Lord is their strength too!

In the Lord I trust with joy,
Amen

CHAPTER 51

Gave

For God so loved the world, that he gave his only begotten
Son, that whosoever believes in him, should not parish but
have everlasting life.

—John 3:16 KJV

God,

You gave it all—
You gave us Jesus!
He gave it all, including his life on the cross.
Lord, what can I give in return?
My belief is that this really happened.
I give you my faith, my hopes, and my heart.
That is all I have . . . it's what I came into the world with,
    and it's how I'm leaving too.
I give you my all.

In God, who gave us all,
I trust,
Amen

CHAPTER 52

Believes

For God so loved the world, that he gave his only begotten Son, that whosoever believes in him, should not parish but have everlasting life.

—John 3:16 KJV

Son of God,

I do believe in you, God. You love us so much, don't you? You believe in us and in this world, even though I really mess things up sometimes. I'm holding on, strong and steady, to the fact that eternal life is mine. God loves us . . . . the God of the universe loves us so much! I believe this fact, now. God, I need to believe in myself too. Please give me confidence to speak this gospel out loud so that others can believe in you and in themselves too.

In God I trust,
Amen

CHAPTER 53

Everything

So no one can become my disciple without giving up everything for me.

—Luke 14:33 NLT

Father in heaven,

Today I have a list . . .

I give you my family.
I give you my friends.
I give you my worries.
I give you my attitudes.
I give you my concerns.
I give you today.
I give you tomorrow.
I give you my earnings.
I give you my job.
I give you my house.
I give you my possessions.
Have I forgotten anything?
Yes, Father,
I give you my heart . . . .
That's everything!

In God I Trust,
Amen

CHAPTER 54

Children

For I rejoiced greatly when brethren came and testified of the truth that is in you, just as you walk in the truth. I have no greater joy than to hear that my children walk in truth.

—3 John 1:3–4 KJV

My heavenly Father,

I am your child. I have parents, and I have children. I wear many hats. Father, today I come to you as a child—your child. I feel squished among all the roles I play in life. It seems like I juggle all these roles, and lately, I've dropped a few. Father, I want to walk in the truth. This is not easy! The world throws many half truths and downright lies at me. Help me to decipher your voice of truth and walk with you, Father, in the direction of peace. Peace, peace . . . Father, I pray for peace. Hearing your voice fills me with comfort. I know you never forsake your children. Father, you are always a prayer away, and I offer this one to you . . . thank you for listening.

> In God, my heavenly Father,
> I trust,
> Amen

CHAPTER 55

Content

> Yet true godliness with contentment is itself great wealth. After all, we brought nothing with us when we came into the world, and we can't take anything with us when we leave it. So if we have enough food and clothing, let us be content.
> —1 Timothy 6:6–8 NLT

Lord,

The world leads me astray when it comes to contentment. It says I need "stuff" to be happy. Lord, help me not to want "stuff." I came into this world with nothing, and I will leave it in the same way. What remains is your Word—that will stay. I find contentment when I pray. The heavier life becomes, the harder I pray. I'm laying my burdens down at the foot of your cross. You lift the burdens of life from my shoulders. I feel lighter, happier . . . content. Thank you, Lord.

In God I trust,
Amen

CHAPTER 56

Trust

Trust in the Lord with all your heart; do not depend on your own understanding. Seek his will in all you do, and he will direct your paths.

—Proverbs 3:5–6 NLT

Lord,

I'm looking at the word "trust." There is a cross at both the beginning and the end of the word. You are the alpha and omega. You know the beginning and the end. You designed humans in your image. You designed me. I trust completely in your plan. You have started great things in my life; I trust in your plan to complete them.

In God alone I trust,
Amen

CHAPTER 57

Control

We all make many mistakes, but those who control their
tongues can also control themselves in every other way.
—James 3:2 NLT

Spirit of God,

What I ask seems simple today:
Be apparent in what I do and say.
Make me think before I talk,
So I both speak the truth and walk the walk.
Words can build up and words can tear down.
Words can bring a smile or bear a frown.
When others try to hurt with their words so searing,
Help me not to be angry and check what I'm hearing.
Maybe they are the ones for whom my prayers
    are needed even more.
Maybe they are lost, insecure, or are keeping some score.
Maybe you're leading me to be an example to them.
When the world rejects, you send me as a friend.
Spirit of God, keep my tongue in control.
I ask this today with my heart and my soul.

In God I trust,
Amen

CHAPTER 58

Eyes

I will lift up mine eyes unto the hills, from whence cometh my help. My help cometh from the Lord, which made heaven and earth.

—Psalm 121:1–2 KJV

Maker of heaven and earth,

I look for you, Lord.
I seek your presence in my life.
Are you there?
Yes, I found you in the eyes, ears, and hugs of friends.
You, Creator, made these eyes of mine, and when they cry,
You send me good people with hearts of gold,
    who cry with me and wipe my tears away.
Yes, Father, I saw you with my own eyes. I looked through
    my own tears and saw you in my friends.
We don't live this life alone.
You created us with eyes that can catch a glimpse of
    heaven here on earth.
I thank you, Creator.
Help me to return this blessing to my friends.
Open my eyes to see their needs as well.

In God we trust,
Amen

CHAPTER 59

Thanks

Give thanks to the Lord, because he is good; his love is eternal.

—Psalm 136:1

To you, Lord, I offer the utmost appreciation.
How do I say it?
A good way is to fold my hands and bow my head.
Next, I
Kneel in your presence and say,
Savior, you alone are God, are good, Love eternally.

In God we trust,
Amen

CHAPTER 60

Together

Where two or three come together in my name, I am there
with them.

—Matthew 18:20

Lord,

When I have the opportunity and privilege to pray or hold
a Bible study, I always set up an extra chair to remind me that,
Lord, you are a very real presence in the place—wherever it is—
that prayers are being uttered. Lord, you are always welcome,
always. Even when I have my prayer time alone, like now, you
are here guiding my pen, and you do so by directing me to the
Bible passages I pick out. Your Word is alive! As I read it and as
generations have before me, I hear Moses, Jeremiah, Paul, and
countless others sharing their stories and your presence. Their
tribute to the trinity is amazing! Your Word is so alive! Help
me to meet together with others to share this fabulous gift.
Whether it is three or two, we meet together to honor you!

In God we two or three trust,
Amen

CHAPTER 61

Determined

Remember that I have commanded you to be determined and confident! Do not be afraid or discouraged, for I the Lord your God, am with you wherever you go.

—Joshua 1:9

Father God,

With you at my side I am determined and confident! My prayer is that you'll help me to keep this positive attitude with me all day today. Whatever it is that lies ahead, it's you and me; together we can face everything and anything that life has to offer. Let there be no trap to trick me, no distractions to unfocus my view of goals, and no voice but yours in my ear.

Give up? No way!
Give in? Not a chance!
Stop trying? never!

In you alone, Father God,
I trust,
Amen

CHAPTER 62

Love

Love is patient and kind; it is not jealous or conceited or proud. Love is not ill mannered or selfish or irritable. Love does not keep a record of wrongs; love is not happy with evil, but is happy with the truth. Love never gives up; and its faith, hope, and patience never fail.

—1 Corinthians 13:4

Jesus,

You, my Friend, are love. I could put your name in this passage in place of the word "love," because you gave your life for me on the cross. That is an immeasurable amount of love! Because you love me that much, I can put my own name in this passage as well. Jesus, help this passage to describe me today. With your help, Jesus, we can make it so.

In Jesus I trust,
Amen

CHAPTER 63

Help

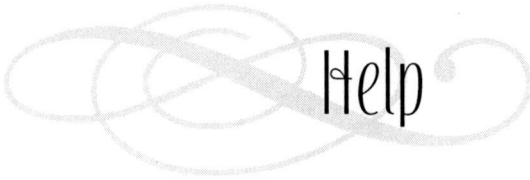

He helps us in all our troubles, so that we are able to help others who have all kinds of troubles, using the same help that we ourselves have received from God.

—2 Corinthians 2:4

Helper,

You give me help—exactly when I need it. All I need to do is ask. My human brain can't always come up with an answer, but you, Father, are already on top of it. Lord, I've never been good at reading maps or finding my way. Some people have the gift of being able to find their way to anywhere. I don't have that gift. I hate being lost—no, I fear being lost. Father, I give this fear to you. Help me get over this "lostness." I ask myself, "What's the worst that could happen?" "I could be a few minutes late" is usually the answer I tell myself, truly, a minor problem when I look at the whole situation. God, you have a GPS (God Plans Specifically) for me. You know where I am, and I wouldn't have it any other way. I'm never lost with you as my guide. Help me to help others focus their GPSs on you as well.

In God who plans specifically
I trust,
Amen

CHAPTER 64

Weakness

But to keep me from being puffed up with pride because of the many wonderful things I saw. I was given a painful physical ailment, which acts as Satan's messenger, to beat me and keep me from being proud. Three times I prayed to the Lord about this and asked him to take it away. But his answer was: "My grace is all you need, for my power is strongest when you are weak," I am most happy, then, to be proud of my weakness in order to feel the protection of Christ's power over me. I am content with weakness, insults, and difficulties for Christ's sake. For when I am weak, then I am strong.

—2 Corinthians 12:7

Lord,

May your strength show through my weakness
    and your power be seen today.
I ask this with all my heart,
    'cuz you answer me when I pray.
"Little ones to him belong,
    we are weak but He is strong"
Were the words we sang to a long-ago song.
But these words still today ring true;
    my hardships I give to you.
What the world will see is you through me.
Because that's what you promise to do!

In God I trust,
Amen

CHAPTER 65

Ability

God has given each of us the ability to do certain things well.

—Romans 12:6 NLT

God,

You have given me the ability to write down prayers; hence, that's why I'm scribbling away. When I write, you fill my brain with endless possibilities. The way I look at words, structure, and cadence of sentences may seem weird to others, but I know you have given me a gift. God, I thank you from my heart! I also have a disability. I can't spell; I never have been able to. Words just don't look wrong, and they are. (Thank you, God, for spell check!) Oh, well, if I focused on my disability, I wouldn't write. Instead I choose to focus on the possibilities. God, I ask to see the possibilities in others—they are created by you. I will reach out, because as you said through Paul in Romans, each of us does *certain* things well. I notice you didn't say *all* things. God, help me to keep this in mind. People need you alone Lord to do all things well.

To God I trust it all,
Amen

CHAPTER 66

King

The Lord is our protector and glorious king, blessing us with kindness and honor. He does not refuse any good thing to those who do what is right. Almighty God, how happy are those who trust in you.

—Psalm 84:11–12

Almighty King,

You are the ruler of heaven and earth. We have earthly rulers; they can't compare to you. We are to obey our earthly rulers, however. From the leaders to the lowest peasant, we acknowledge you alone as the King of kings. Lord, today I pray for all those who lead. May they trust in our heavenly King, who gave them their gift of leadership in the first place. If they trust in you, then I trust in them. Like it says on the penny . . .

In God we trust,
Amen

CHAPTER 67

Forgive

You are the people of God; he loves you and chose you for his own. So then you must clothe yourself in with compassion, kindness, humility, gentleness and patience. Be tolerant of one another and forgive one another whenever any of you has a complaint against someone else.

—Colossians 3:12–13

God,

> When I see pain on someone's face,
> May my compassion take its place.
> When a friend's actions betray,
> May my kindness make her day.
> When the pompousness of the proud
> Comes to my ears out loud,
> May the humility of your Spirit
> Dampen the noise so I don't hear it.
> When situations get rough,
> May your gentle Spirit speak,
> "Enough is enough."
> And when my will gets ahead,
> Grant me patience to forgive instead.

> In God we trust,
> Amen

CHAPTER 68

Power

> Shadrach, Meshach and Abednego replied to the king, "O
> Nebuchadnezzar, we do not need to defend ourselves before
> you in this matter. If we are thrown into the blazing furnace,
> the God we serve is able to save us from it, and he will rescue
> us from your hand, O king."
> —Daniel 3:16–17 NIV

God,

I know the end of this story; I learned it in Sunday school long ago. By your power, you saved these three men from certain death in the flames of a fiery furnace. An angel appeared with them. Lord, angels are your messengers. I wonder if I've seen any lately. I can only imagine what it was like at the time of Daniel, when these men were punished for being believers in you. Wait, believers are being persecuted all over the globe! God, I forget this. I worship with such freedom. Help me to never take this for granted. Lord, by your power, I am able to be a faithful believer and be proud of being a Christian. Help me to be aware of your power every day in my life. The power of the deadly furnace couldn't singe a hair on the heads of these three believers. Your power protects your kingdom. Help me to be a powerful participant in your kingdom, side by side with the angels, who worship you in heaven.

In God I trust,
Amen

CHAPTER 69

Happen

> Everything that happens in this world happens at the time God chooses . . . . Whatever happens or can happen has already happened before. God makes the same thing happen again and again.
>
> —Ecclesiastes 3:1, 15

Father,

We find so much comfort in the fact that you are in control. Also, many of the troubles we are facing today are troubles that other saints have experienced before us. Our children have much to look forward to, because you are in our future. God, you know the ending to this story, and so do we. It will happen—heaven is our family's home.

> In God we trust to make this
> happen,
> Amen

CHAPTER 70

Hearts

That is why the Lord says, "Turn to me now, while there is time! Give me your hearts."

—Joel 2:12 NLT

Lord,

I have given you my heart. I gave it to you long ago. The problem is that I need to be reminded of your presence; I think I can do it on my own. Lord, I turn to you now, offering my heart—it is my present. You return the gift with your presence, always. Thank you for never abandoning me. I will never turn away from you. Help me, Lord, to turn away from the sins and offerings of this world; they present me with nothing that lasts. You, Lord, offer salvation for eternity. My heart has a limited amount of beats here on earth. I don't know how many, but you do, Lord. I want my every heartbeat to beat in time with your eternal plan. Earthly time as we know it is running short. I will keep my earthly heart in shape, and through studying your Word, I'll keep my spiritual heart in shape too.

> In God I trust with all
> my heart,
> Amen

CHAPTER 71

Sing

The Lord your God is with you, his power gives you victory. The Lord will take delight in you, and his love will give you new life. He will sing and be joyful over you.

—Zephaniah 3:17

Lord,

I never thought about *you* singing. I've thought of angels singing at Jesus' birth, Paul singing in prison, and King David writing all the psalms and setting them to music. All human talent comes from you—we are your creation. All creation praises you, Lord. Yet I want to think about this . . . you, Lord, will be joyful over me? Father, will you sing a soulful ballad or a powerful song with a rock-n-roll beat? Lord, can we dance together in heaven? Can we sing a joyful song together someday? Until then, Father, I will treasure the joy of music and dancing with the people I love.

> In God I trust to sing
> my life's song,
> Amen

CHAPTER 72

Peace

Lord, I have given up my pride and turned away from my arrogance. I am not concerned with great matters or with subjects too difficult for me. Instead, I am content and at peace. As a child lies quietly in its mother's arms, so my heart is quiet within me.

—Psalm 131:1–2

Lord,

I will get **rid** of **pride**. May it be replaced with **peace**.

In God we trust,
Amen

CHAPTER 73

Builds

Then we shall no longer be children, carried by the waves and blown about by every shifting wind of teaching by deceitful men, who lead others into error by the tricks they invent. Instead, by speaking the truth in the spirit of love we must grow up in every way to Christ, who is the head. Under his control all the different parts of the body fit together, and the whole body is held together by joint with which it is provided. So when each separate part works as is should, the whole body grows and builds itself up through love.

—Ephesians 4:14–16

Christ,

You are the leader of the body, the body of the church. When all parts are working as they should, we build one another up and grow stronger through love. Lord, help me to be a body builder—not in the physical sense, but in a spiritual one. So many forces work against the church—they are all of the enemy's doing. He annoys and destroys, but in you, Christ, we are filled up and built up. You love us so much. Help us to be joined together in love; for in this way we are a healthy church, where young and old can continue to grow in faith.

> In Christ we trust to lead His church,
> Amen

CHAPTER 74

Speak

Lord, you have examined me and know me. You know everything I do; from far away you understand all my thoughts. You see me whether I am working or resting; you know my actions even before I speak you already know what I will say. You are around me on every side; you protect me with your power.

—Psalm 139:1–5

Lord,

I spoke today . . . I spoke up. I had friends pray for me before I spoke. I actually got a bit teary during my speech. I wasn't embarrassed . . . no, it was you, Lord. You made me see through the tears and not lose my composure. I kept going. I spoke of my story. I spoke of my faith. I wished I could have said more. If I have the opportunity, Lord, you will prepare me for it. Lord, please continue to use me in this manner. I am ready, willing, and able to speak your truth. I'm ready for another assignment. Bring it on.

> In God I trust to help me
> speak up,
> Amen

CHAPTER 75

Treasure

Yet we who have this spiritual treasure are like common clay pots, in order to show that the supreme power belongs to God, not to us.

—2 Corinthians 4:7

Holy One,

Clay pots were used in Bible times to store things. Today it's Tupperware. Tupperware and its copycats are nondescript, semi-disposable, lookalike, reusable containers. But they keep what's inside from spoiling. On the outside we are all just clay pots, but inside we all house a treasure. That spiritual treasure is how you made us all unique, living, breathing people who treasure you in our hearts. Holy Spirit, keep us fresh in this stale world. We may all look the same as Tupperware on the outside, but we are each uniquely gifted from you. We have a treasure that the world doesn't have . . . and that's you, the living God we treasure.

In God we trust,
Amen

CHAPTER 76

Rainbow

When the rainbow appears in the clouds, I will see it and remember the everlasting covenant between me and all living beings on earth.

—Genesis 9:16

God,

Red
Amber
Indigo
Noah saw the first one!
Blue
Orange
White

You said you'd never send a flood again like the flood in Noah's time. Lord, what about all the other disasters that seem to be happening all over the globe? I've never understood this, Lord. Maybe I'm not supposed to. I'm just supposed to give help when I can to those in need. I will show your love and offer what I can to those who have lost so much.

Ready to help.
Always lend a hand.
Invite a friend.
Never turn away.
Be there.
Offer time.
Which way, Lord?

> In God I trust to keep his
> promise,
> Amen

CHAPTER 77

Nothing

For I am certain that nothing can separate us from his love: neither death nor life, neither angels nor other heavenly rulers or powers, neither the world above, nor the world below—there is nothing in all creation that will ever be able to separate us from the love of God which is ours through Christ Jesus.

—Romans 8:38–39

Jesus,

You connect us to our heavenly Father. Sometimes it is me who is the willful and ornery one. I separate myself from you by not listening to your quiet voice. Jesus, I come to you earnestly in my prayers today. Let nothing separate me from you. I hold on to you and you to me in an embrace that nothing can separate. Help me to tell others how they can have this relationship with you. Some days we have mountaintop experiences; some days we struggle in the valleys. It does not matter what the day brings because you are with me (with us).

> In Jesus I trust to stay
> connected,
> Amen

CHAPTER 78

Cloak

And everywhere Jesus went, to villages, towns, or farms, people would take their sick to the market places and beg him to let the sick at least touch the edge of his cloak. And all who touched it were made well.

—Mark 6:56

Jesus,

I come today asking only to touch the edge of your cloak. I'm not feeling very well. This frustrates me because I have things to do. Wait. I just need to spend time in your presence and rest. I need to slow down and be filled. How will I go out in the world and be effective unless I touch your cloak first? Jesus, when your feet touched roads here on earth, your words touched so many. Your Word still continues to touch us. I see your words in the gospel, and I feel I'm touching your cloak. Renew, refresh, recharge, rejoice!

In Jesus I trust,
Amen

CHAPTER 79

Test

Every test that you have experienced is the kind that normally comes to people. But God keeps his promise, and he will not allow you to be tested beyond your power to remain firm; at the time you are put to the test he will give you the strength to endure it, and so provide you with a way out.
—1 Corinthians 10:13

Lord,

Can this test be done? I want to hand in my paper now. I didn't cheat. I didn't look at someone else's life for the answers, but instead I turned to your Word. This is an open book test, and I found 1 Corinthians 10:13. Like this passage says, we will be able to endure, won't we? I feel like I'm slowing down—my endurance is waning. The only way is if I hand it to you, Lord. I can see my work is incomplete (and you, Lord have never stopped working patiently and consistently in my life.) OK, I'll take it back and work on it some more; there's more to be learned here. Teacher, thank you for being patient.

In God, who teaches me life's
lessons, I trust,
Amen

CHAPTER 80

Result

My brothers, consider yourselves fortunate when all kinds of trials come your way, for you know that when your faith succeeds in facing such trials, the result is your ability to endure. Make sure that your endurance carries with you all the way without failing, so that you may be perfect, and complete, lacking nothing.

—James 1:2–4

Lord,

I'm starting to understand now . . . . I have a lot to learn, don't I? These trials in life are not going to end, are they? No, as long as I'm alive, they will be with me. Lord, the result of this testing should be—no, will be a stronger faith. Yes, that's the result. You are the ultimate teacher. I am so fortunate to be in your class in life!

In God I trust,
Amen

CHAPTER 81

Secrets

The maker of heaven and earth—the Lord is thy name—
says this: Ask me and I will tell you some remarkable secrets
about what is going to happen here.

—Jeremiah 33:2–3

Lord,

When I think of a friend telling me a secret, I picture
someone cupping my ear in her hand and whispering softly.
The key is to listen. I pray for better listening abilities—my
hearing is fine; for this I am thankful. I pray that you increase
my listening habits. Lord, I want to really absorb what I hear
and take time to respond to others. My first step in acquiring
this skill is to practice listening to my friend who constantly
tells me things. You speak to my heart, Lord. Friend, tell me a
secret.

In God I trust to put the
answer in the ears of my heart,
Amen

CHAPTER 82

Find

Try to find out what is pleasing to the Lord.

—Ephesians 5:10

Lord,

What brings a smile to your face?
I will try today to see
What person, time, event, or place
You find, Lord, to smile through me!

Amen

near

But as for me, how wonderful it is to be near God, to find protection with the Lord God and to proclaim all he has done!

—Psalm 73:28

Lord God,

In order to draw near to you, I need to be quiet. I need to stop thrashing about in my life. I have a desire to be moving constantly: doing my job, carting kids around, running errands, watching the clock. I need to step back from this merry-go-round. I need to get off this ride!

Whew!

Quiet . . . stillness . . . calmness . . . peace.

Lord, as I look back at my life, I see and appreciate what you've accomplished! I see and give you so much praise for what you've done. You've been there through good times and bad. Lord, I draw near to you simply to say "thank you." Thank you for being there to protect me, guide me, catch me, encourage me, test me, and simply love me.

In God I trust to be near me
always,
Amen

CHAPTER 84

Remembered

Mary remembered all these things and thought deeply about them.

—Luke 2:19

Jesus,

If you'd been born today, Lord, I bet your mother, Mary, would have made a great scrapbook of your life. As a mother, she held her memories so dear. I picture the manger and the animals that were present at your birth. I picture Joseph, proudly protecting his young family as you fled from Herod. I picture your first steps and first words—she remembered all these things. Jesus, I wish more details were recorded in the Bible about you growing up. As parents, we do remember and reminisce about these milestones.

But the end of your earthly life was, of course, very painful. Your mother was at the foot of the cross. My heart cannot even begin to bear what Mary's did! Jesus, please bless my parents. May they be remembered fondly and with love. Jesus, help me always to appreciate them and what they did for me.

In Jesus, Mary's Son, I trust,
Amen

Grow

Dear brothers and sisters, whenever trouble comes your way, let it be an opportunity for joy. For when your faith is tested, your endurance has a chance to grow.

—James 1:2–3 NLT

Holy God,

I stand before you as a seedling, a tiny tree. I used to be just an acorn. Someday, with your help, I'll grow into a mighty oak. But until then, I will have to stay rooted firmly in you, Lord, because some days will be stormy or windy or icy or scorching or freezing or sunny or rainy. No matter how life tests me, my faith will grow deeper in you. I see all these conditions as tests—tests to help me grow stronger. Here's the hardest part though, Lord, "opportunity for joy," you say? I get so bogged down with my testing that I forget the joy part. Help me, Lord, never to forget to grow in joy. Frankly, my words are deceiving. I'm really having trouble finding joy right now, Lord! I'm not doing this well tonight, am I, Lord? I'll put my pen down— help me tomorrow, okay?

> In God I trust with
> my tomorrow,
> Amen

Grow

Dear brothers and sisters, whenever trouble comes your way, let it be an opportunity for joy. For when your faith is tested, your endurance has a chance to grow.

—James 1:2–3 NLT

Lord,

There are amazing stories of fellow brothers and sisters in Christ overcoming huge obstacles and living their lives in total adherence to your will. Lord, I thank you for these heroes of the faith—all of them. I wish I could be like them. Sometimes, I feel like I can't even handle the little stuff, you know, the little frustrations and irritants that come my way. Lord, I have a lot of growing to do. Growing up, that is. Age rightly has nothing to do with it. Lord, I want to stay deeply rooted in you alone, so that we can endure together. The result will be joy, as you help me and all of our family of believers through this.

In God I trust to help
me grow,
Amen

Grow

Dear brothers and sisters, whenever trouble comes your way, let it be an opportunity for joy. For when your faith is tested, your endurance has a chance to grow.

—James 1:2–3 NLT

Holy God,

I think I've found that joy now. I've read this passage from James 1:23 over and over. You are teaching me about how to grow in joy: the only way is to endure trouble! Over the last twenty-four hours my faith was tested. The evil one was blocking my reasoning in understanding this passage as well as with other issues in my life. I wanted to believe it, live it, but I stumbled over my own feet, and I compared myself to others, wanting their faith, wishing I could be like them.

You have given me another chance—thank you, God! I have endured this test! It was my own thoughts and defeated attitude that made me think I'm not good enough. Holy One, I still don't understand it all, and I never will, but I'm learning. The roots of my faith never gave way, even though the winds of trouble tried to change my mind and direction. This was a test of my mind. Help me to grow in faith so that, having learned from this trouble, I'm even more prepared and stronger for tomorrow. Bring tomorrow on—I'm ready!

In God I trust to grow
and endure,
Amen

CHAPTER 86

Letter

You yourselves are our letter, written on our hearts, known and read by everybody. You show that you are a letter from Christ, the result of our ministry, written not with ink but with the Spirit of the living God, not on tablets of stone but on tablets of human hearts.

—2 Corinthians 3:2–3

Dear Holy Spirit,

You are the one who makes me able to communicate with the Father. I don't need to dial 1-800-HOL-YGOD or e-mail jesusisrisen@gmail.com to know that my God is alive and well. I hear you and see you with the eyes and ears of my heart. Technology is fast, but, Holy One, you are faster. Computers hold so much information, but your Word is truth. The language of prayer has no dialects. Holy Spirit, you understand them all. Help me to live by your Word alone, seeing, hearing, and living with your Holy Spirit in my heart, your personal letter to me.

In God I trust with every beat
of my heart,
Amen

CHAPTER 87

Sanctuary

I entered the sanctuary of God.

—Psalm 73:17

Lord,

In your sanctuary, I find rest for my weary soul. Sometimes you provide a sanctuary in my friends and family, yet sometimes I need to be alone. No matter, I seek peace, your peace; whether it fills a church or a group of people or if I'm alone. Jesus, I desire quiet rest and reflection. I take a deep breath, I let it out slowly . . . .

I let go of all today's worries and regrets
I let go of fear that's holding me back
I let go of past failures
I let God take my worries away
I let God calm my fears
I let God have today
God, you are already in my future. You know what will happen, and it's all under your divine control. Thank you. Praise God!
Now . . .
Let's go, God!

In God I trust as I enter and
exit this sanctuary,
Amen

CHAPTER 88

Death

Death is swallowed up in victory. O death, where is your victory? O death, where is your sting?

—1 Corinthians 15:54–55 NLT

Jesus,

You went through personally and conquered eternally . . . death. How many "thank yous" can I say? My words seem so . . . I don't know, meager, not enough. I personally, and all those I know and love must go through death too. Lord, because of your death and resurrection, I too will conquer death. The sting in my heart when someone dies is only the brokenness I feel now that he or she is gone from this earth, from my world. Now, Jesus, you hold (this person) in your arms. I look forward to the day when I can meet all the saints who've gone before me. I'm not afraid, Jesus. It'll be like a huge reunion, and what a party it will be! The sting of death may sadden my heart, but it won't overwhelm it, Lord. We'll get through this. I know because . . .

In God we trust,
Amen

CHAPTER 89

Trouble

The Lord is good; he protects his people in times of trouble;
He takes care of those who turn to him.

—Nahum 1:7

Father,

I feel like all my friends and family are having an inordinate and unfair amount of trouble right now. I can't make all these troubles go away; all I can do is point them in the right direction, and that's to you! Father, I come to you, broken and hurt. I'm in need of a hug from my heavenly Father, I know you care for all your children and you love them as only our heavenly Father can love. I trust you have all of us and our situations under control, even though they are very troubling to all of us right now.

In you alone, Father, we put
our trust,
Amen

(Father, remember how I found the first penny when I didn't know what was going on with MS? I found another penny in the street today. You are an awesome God. I needed that affirmation. Thank you.)

CHAPTER 90

Patiently

But if we look forward to something we don't have yet, we
must wait patiently and confidently.

—Romans 8:25 NLT

Lord,

So many days I search in vain for answers to my problems
that weigh me down. So many nights I cry myself to sleep.
(Wow! Lord, don't I sound like a barrel of fun?) I'm currently
not a great person to be around. I've sunk to the depths. Lord,
it's time for a change. I need to wait confidently for your light
and presence in my life's situations. You never leave us nor
forsake us. I need to look forward to and trust in your answers
that are yet to be revealed.

Problems
Are
The
Ignition to
Every
New
Triumph. To
Learn,
You must

Wait on the Lord,
and trust in him.
Amen

CHAPTER 91

You Pick a Word

I waited patiently for the Lord's help; then he listened to me and heard my cry. He pulled me out of a dangerous pit, out of deadly quicksand. He set me safely on a rock and made me secure. He taught me to sing a new song, a song of praise to our God. Many who see this will take warning and will put their trust in the Lord.

—Psalm 40:1–3

Lord,

I cannot even begin to rewrite these beautiful words of David. I cannot add to or take away from them. Lord, all I can do is wait patiently for you! I try so hard sometimes to do things that I think are helpful, when all I am really doing is spinning my wheels in quicksand. I hope, I pray, I trust in what you're accomplishing through these prayers. I pray that all who read your Word, Father, not mine, will come to put their trust in you. That's really what it's all about.

In God we trust,
Amen

Hope

Why am I so sad? Why am I so troubled? I will put my hope in God.

—Psalms 42:5; 42:11; 43:5

Lord,

Why, why, why? There is no answer. I will

Hold
On
Patiently
Endure

Why? Because
In God we trust,
Amen

Shield

The Lord is my strength and shield; my heart trusts in him, and I am helped. My heart leaps for joy and I will give thanks to him in song.

—Psalm 28:7

(I have found three pennies lately—in the dirt, on the road, and in an unused handbag. Lord, nine more prayers—that's what I need to complete this task you've set before me. Thy will be done.)

Lord,

Many days I feel like going into battle. I feel like I'm fighting—fighting some days simply for clarity of my thoughts. I'm constantly distracted, and I want only to bring a task to completion. Maybe, Lord, the reason I'm having trouble finishing is that you didn't assign me all these tasks in the first place. I'm doing what the demands of my life are calling me to do, and I'm not listening to what my heavenly Father is telling me. Father, today I ask for protection:

Shield me from unproductive business.
Shield me from the clock and time constraints.
Shield me from a quick temper.
Shield me from the need for things.
Shield me from the world.

Wait, Lord, I'm in the world but not of the world. Why do I feel like all these arrows are aimed right at me today? I need to trust in the strength of this shield; it's my faith in you, and it's being tested. Can you help me to hold up this shield today? Let's do it together. There, the weight is lighter when I let you help me carry it, Lord. In fact, I'm going to let go now. I give you this weight of the world on my heart. Thank you, Father. Shield me from thinking that I can handle all this on my own, today and tomorrow as well.

In God I trust,
Amen

CHAPTER 94

Want

"Father," he prayed. "My Father! All things are possible for you. Take this cup of suffering away from me. Yet not what I want, but what you want."

—Mark 14:36

Jesus,

This is your ultimate prayer in the garden of Gethsemane. You prayed it not once, not twice, but three times. (See Mark 14:32–42.)

The answer?
You followed through, and so did your Father. For our heavenly Father, all things are possible. He could have made the whole situation go away, but he didn't. My salvation depended on that. Jesus, what you went through my human brain cannot even fathom. What do I want, Jesus? I want you to know how much I love you for what you did. What do I want, Father? Only for you to know how much I love you for what you didn't do.

In God I trust with my wants,
Amen

CHAPTER 95

Turn

The Lord is good; he protects his people in times of trouble;
he takes care of those who turn to him.

—Nahum 1:7

Lord,

Oh, Lord, you are so good! You are my protection, through
the rough times and stormy seas. You take care of me. What is
my response? I turn to you for help. It's going to take a physical
and spiritual change in direction, and I trust in you to be my
compass and map. Show me the way. Be the captain of this
ship.

In God I trust,
Amen

CHAPTER 96

Lose

Whoever tries to gain his own life will lose it; but whoever loses his life for my sake will gain it.

—Matthew 10:39

Jesus,

You lost your life for me. I need to lose my life as well. Help me, Jesus, to do this. The world dazzles, beckons, bewilders, distracts, betrays, and ultimately, could destroy. But because of what you did, I too will look only at you and your will for me. You never said this would be easy; in fact, this is the most critical thing I've ever done. I give you my life. Live through me; saturate my heart with your will. Envelop me in your plans; use my life to affect others. Help me to see through your eyes what needs to be done so that others will see you, precious Jesus. You've made me a winner by being a loser.

In Jesus I trust,
Amen

CHAPTER 97

Fathers

Have you forgotten the encouraging words when God speaks to you his sons, "My son, pay close attention when the Lord corrects you, and do not be discouraged when he rebukes you. Because the Lord corrects every one he loves, and punishes every one he accepts as his son. Endure what you suffer as being a father's punishment; your suffering shows that God is treating you as his sons.

—Hebrews 12:5–6

Father,

I remember standing on my father's feet, with my own on top, learning to dance, when I was very young. I remember hearing Glen Miller playing on a record on a stereo. I also remember the punishment he dealt out when I talked back to my mother. I remember my dad teaching me how to drive, how to land a fish, and then how to take the fish off the hook. I remember him walking me down the aisle. I remember my dad holding my daughter as a tiny, day-old baby. I thought he'd never let her go. I remember how my father taught my son how to fish and fly remote control planes. Heavenly Father, a heartfelt thank you for my earthly father. My earthly father's in my heavenly Father's hands.

In God we trust,
Amen

CHAPTER 98

Walking

It was faith that made Jacob bless each of the sons of Joseph just before he died. He leaned on the top of his walking stick and worshiped God.

—Hebrews 11:21

God,

Do I lean on you too much?
Do I want you to take it all away? All the troubles, that is.
Do I think life should be trouble free?
Do I think I can handle this all on my own?
Am I stubborn and prideful?
Am I fiercely independent?

God, I yearn to be walking on the paths you have planned for me. I'm asking for your help and guidance. I need to lean on you, Lord; be my walking stick. Lord, help me to recognize your help. Sometimes your "walking stick" comes in the form of other people who have been down this particular path already. And in the same manner, help my life walk with you, Lord, to be a help to others. You have always been there for me, never left my side, walking with me. God, help me to be there for whomever you have me meet on life's journey.

> In God I trust, walking with
> me every day,
> Amen

CHAPTER 99

Almighty

When I am afraid, O Lord Almighty, I put my trust in you. I trust in God and am not afraid. I praise him for what he has promised. What can a mere human being do to me?
—Psalm 56:3–4

Almighty God,

What can humans do to me? A lot is what I say! God, I'm sometimes afraid of crime, the future, my health, my family's health, my job, chemicals, nuclear war, ozone, aging, making a mistake, forgetting something, criticism of friends, not being a good enough friend, making the grade, being late, wars, famine, disease . . . .

Okay—sorry, Lord. I went off on a tangent there. It did actually help to write all those down. When I look at this list I think, *Hmmm, what do I really have control of?* Not much! You know, I will just hand all this over to you, Lord. You handle it all, because you are All-mighty.

In the Almighty God I trust,
Amen

CHAPTER 100

Judges

But the Lord said to him, "Pay no attention to how tall and handsome he is. I have rejected him, because I do not judge as a man judges. Man looks at the outward appearance, but I look at the heart."

—1 Samuel 16:7

Lord God,

In a world that judges us in human terms by looks, income, or fame, I'm glad you look only at my heart. Wait a minute—I think I ought to do a little housecleaning of sorts there too. Today, Father, help me to see people as Jesus sees them; open the eyes of my heart to look past the physical and to throw away prejudice. There is no room in my heart for that. You are the only judge. Purify my heart, and may it show outwardly in my attitude.

In the God who judges us all
I trust to make this happen
for me today,
Amen

CHAPTER 101

Prayer

Therefore I tell you, whatever you ask for in prayer, believe that you have received it, and it will be yours.

—Mark 11:24

Jesus,

You are not a God who looks at prayer like a grocery list—that's not how it works. Your timing is perfect. I have complete trust in your timing in my life. My faith in your plan makes things possible but not always easy. If we gave everything to our children that they wanted, they'd be nothing but spoiled brats. There are times, though, that I don't see you working in my life directly. You may be working totally behind the scenes right now, in fact. My prayer is this: may I have complete faith in your plan, even when it seems invisible to me.

In God I trust,
Amen

A Finale Prayer of Praise

Praise God in his temple!
Praise his strength in heaven!
Praise him for the mighty things he has done.
Praise his supreme greatness.
Praise him with trumpets.
Praise him with harps and lyres.
Praise him with drums and dancing.
Praise him with harps and flutes.
Praise him with cymbals.
Praise him with loud cymbals.
Praise the Lord, all living creatures!
Praise the Lord!

—Psalm 150

When notes are strung together, they form a perfect tone.
The notes of a chord are played together,
    no one can stand alone.
The staff that the notes sit upon gives each one a place.
In time and with time each envelops
    the uniqueness of its space.
The harmonies life offers us are as varied as
    each person's thoughts.
If only people worked together like chords,
Knowing what wonderful melodies they brought.
To live, to love, to laugh together, oh,
    what melodies could be.
Life would be an endless song played by and for you and me.
Now, sometimes the harmonies would be happy,
At other times they might bring tears.
Sometimes songs are short and sweet,
And some compositions take years.
We are all composers of sorts, directing
    the sounds of our lives.
We try and try to make it all sound right,
    and for perfection each strives.
Now, what we all are forgetting here,
    in achieving perfect sound,
Is the one who's the real conductor.
    And where is he to be found?
Why, He's in our hearts, and He responds to every beat.
But He doesn't keep time, He has no baton,
And someday we'll get to meet.
The master of creation, the maestro of it all,
The one who composed all of life's song—
We'll meet him someday, along with the saints,
And together we'll all sing along.
Until that day we'll just have to stay,
    marching along with the band.

Keeping in time and harmony, doing the best that we can.
To remember who created our hearts that keep time even
    though we forget,
The maestro who created them, He's the best musician
    yet!

—by Nancy Roberts

(If King David could complete the Book of Psalms with
this beautiful song of praise to our Lord, then I can take his
example and end this collection of prayers with a poem of
praise to our Lord as well.)

So now you have one dollar and one penny's worth of prayers. As I reread and rewrote this manuscript, the numbers kept being off. My intent was to write one hundred prayers, but as I wrote I found out I had two prayers highlighting the word "hope." How could I take out a prayer on hope just to make my numbers work out right? I figure that someone out there needs more hope; I know I do! Also, prayer 101, another "extra" is on the very essence of what this is about; again, how could I omit it? Life is not perfect, oh well . . . .

There is nothing magical about the words I've written, but there's empowerment in the Word itself—the living Word of our Lord. He wants to speak with you. He wants to spend time with you. He is your friend. Trust in him. The next time you happen to find a penny, or any change for that matter, think about trusting in God. Talk to Him, and then quiet yourself to listen for His answer. He's an amazing God: know it, feel it, believe it, hear it, and trust Him to make cents of it all.

In God we trust,
Amen

CPSIA information can be obtained at www.ICGtesting.com
Printed in the USA
BVOW022253171011

273878BV00001B/83/P